From A to Z

Copyright © 1979, Grisewood and Dempsey

All rights reserved. No part of this book may be
reproduced or utilized in any form or by any means,
electronic or mechanical, including photocopying,
recording, or by any information storage and retrieval
system, without permission in writing from the Publisher.
Inquiries should be addressed to Raintree Childrens Books,
205 West Highland Avenue, Milwaukee, Wisconsin 53203.

Library of Congress Number: 78-21027

2 3 4 5 6 7 8 9 0 83 82 81 80 79

Printed in the United States of America.

Library of Congress Cataloging in Publication Data

Manley, Deborah.
  From A to Z.

  SUMMARY: Brief text and illustrations introduce
the alphabet.
  1. English language — Alphabet — Juvenile litera-
ture. [1. Alphabet] I. Kailer-Lowndes (Firm)
II. Title.
PE1155.M36 [E] 78-21027
ISBN 0-8172-1303-1 lib. bdg.

From A to Z

Words by
Deborah Manley

Pictures by
Kailer/Lowndes

RAINTREE CHILDRENS BOOKS
Milwaukee · Toronto · Melbourne · London

A is the first letter of the alphabet. Airplane starts with the letter **A**. Have you ever taken a ride in an airplane?

This boat has many sails. Count
the people on the boat.

Cc

The castle has many towers.
How many towers are there?
Which tower is the highest?

Dd

What letter does dragon
start with?

E e

There is a seat on the back of
the elephant. Would you like to
take a ride on an elephant?

F f

These flowers are called roses. What colors are the roses? How many roses are there?

G g

What is the giraffe doing? How does being tall help the giraffe?

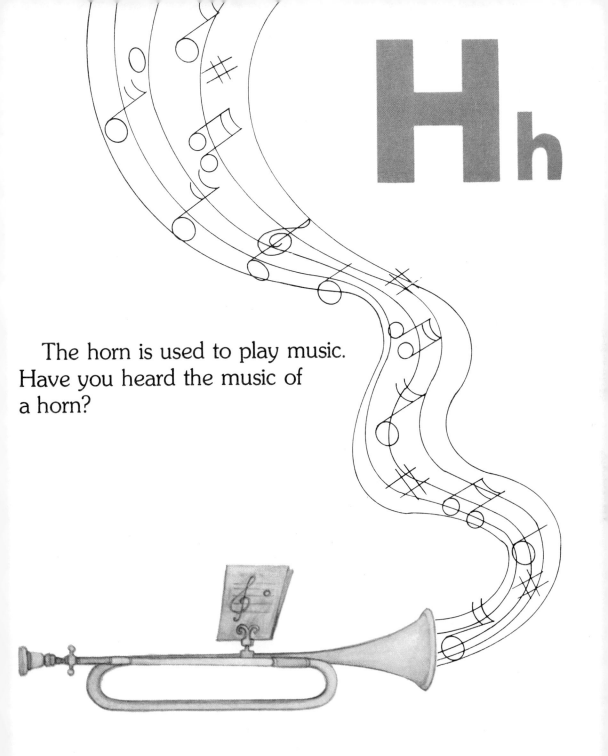

Hh

The horn is used to play music.
Have you heard the music of
a horn?

Ii

An island is land with water all around it. Do you know the name of any islands?

Jj

The juggler keeps several balls
moving in the air at the same time.
How many balls are in the air?

Kk

Here is a mother kangaroo and her baby. How does the mother kangaroo carry the baby kangaroo?

The lion is a kind of cat. Does the lion look like cats you have seen?

Mm

The word mountain begins with
the letter **M**. Can you think of
other words that begin with **M**?

Nn

The bird is in its nest. What else is in the nest?

O o

What color is the fruit of the orange tree? How many oranges are on the tree?

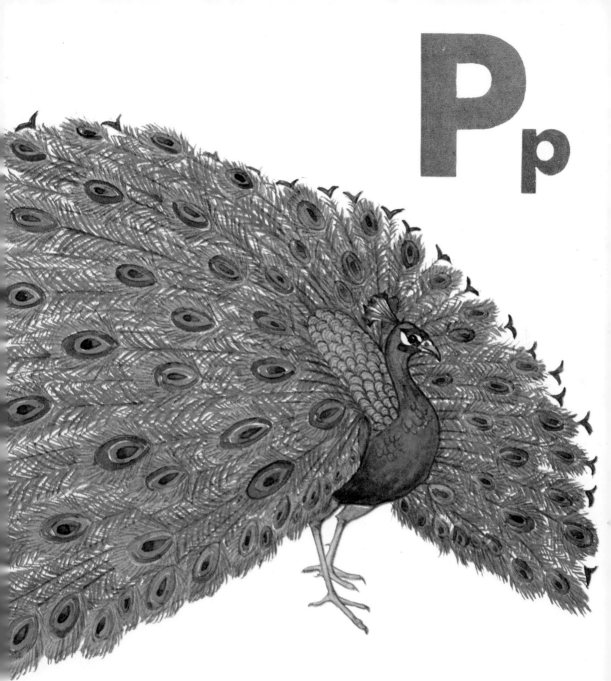

P p

The peacock is a bird with long beautiful feathers. What colors are the feathers?

Qq

Here are four babies. Four of the very same thing are called quadruplets.

The feather in the soldier's hat is red. Which other parts of his clothing are red?

S s

This animal moves along the ground without any legs. What is its name?

T t

The train has three cars. How many people can you see on the train?

U u

The unicorn is an imaginary animal. Can you name other imaginary animals?

The village is built on the side of a mountain. Find the highest building in the village.

Ww

Wigwams are made of poles covered with animal skins, leaves, or bark. Do you know who lived in wigwams? Would you like to live in a wigwam?

Have you ever heard the music of a xylophone? Each key is a different color. How many keys are there?

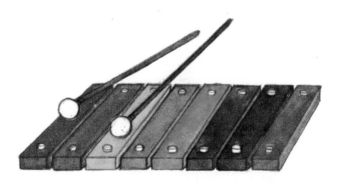

What color is the sun? What
letter does the color start with?

Z z

Sometimes a zebra has brown stripes, and sometimes it has black stripes. What color is this zebra's stripes?

This will help you with the Word Review.

a	**a** as in **cat**
ā	**a** as in **able**
ä	**a** as in **father**
e	**e** as in **bend**
ē	**e** as in **me**
i	**i** as in **in**
ī	**i** as in **ice**
o	**o** as in **top**
ō	**o** as in **old**
ô	**o** as in **cloth**
o͞o	**oo** as in **good**
o͞o	**oo** as in **tool**
oi	**oi** as in **oil**
ou	**ou** as in **out**
u	**u** as in **up**
ur	**ur** as in **fur**
yo͞o	**u** as in **use**
ə	**a** as in **again**
ch	**ch** as in **such**
ng	**ng** as in **sing**
sh	**sh** as in **shell**
th	**th** as in **three**
th	**th** as in **that**

Word Review

Here are some words in *From A to Z.* Practice saying each word out loud. See if you can find them in the book.

alphabet (al′ fə bet′)
feather (fe<u>th</u>′ ər)
giraffe (jə raf′)
island (ī′ lənd)
juggler (jug′ ə lər)
kangaroo (kang′ gə rōō′)
peacock (pē′ kok′)
quadruplet (kwä drōōp′ lət)
rose (rōz)
soldier (sōl′ jər)
unicorn (yōō′ nə kôrn′)
village (vil′ ij)
wigwam (wig′ wom)
xylophone (zī′ lə fōn′)
zebra (zē′ brə)